CALLED TO BE HOLY

The Discipline of the Church

Jeremy Walker

THE BANNER OF TRUTH TRUST

THE BANNER OF TRUTH TRUST

Head Office
3 Murrayfield Road
Edinburgh, EH12 6EL
UK

North America Office
610 Alexander Spring Road
Carlisle, PA 17015
USA

banneroftruth.org

© The Banner of Truth 2023

*

ISBN
Print: 978 1 80040 320 8
Epub: 978 1 80040 321 5
Kindle: 978 1 80040 322 2

*

Typeset in Adobe Garamond Pro 10.5/13.5 at
The Banner of Truth Trust, Edinburgh.

Printed in the UK by
Buchanan McPherson Ltd.,
Hamilton.

Unless otherwise indicated, all Scripture quotations are taken from the
New King James Version. Copyright © 1982 by Thomas Nelson Inc.
Used by permission. All rights reserved.

CALLED TO BE HOLY:
THE DISCIPLINE OF THE CHURCH

THE church is a gracious and glorious creation of the sovereign God. She has been called out of the world as the special treasure and particular delight of the Lord God Almighty. The church is summoned by the true God. It is made alive in Christ, united to him, distinct from those who are not his people, ordered in accordance with God's will, and blessed in all her relationships to him. The good news of Christ Jesus who died and rose and ascended for his people comes to ungodly men and women with saving power and they are changed in the depths of their being.

The classic sequence is described for us in Acts 18:8, where this gospel comes to Corinth by the mouth of Paul, the Lord's apostle. Paul preaches in Corinth that Jesus is the Christ, first to Jews and then to Gentiles, 'and many of the Corinthians, hearing, believed and were baptised.' When God's powerful call came, these sinners were drawn to the Lord Jesus in faith. They identified themselves with their Redeemer in baptism as those washed, sanctified, and justified, through the Spirit's agency (1 Cor. 6:11). By virtue of this process, these believers could then be written to and described by the apostle in the following language: 'To the church of God which is at Corinth, to those who are sanctified in Christ Jesus, called to be saints, with all who in every place call on the name of Jesus Christ our Lord, both theirs and ours' (1 Cor. 1:2).

In short, this process of hearing, believing, and being baptised, resulted in a group of people who could be described as a local church, 'the church of God which is at Corinth.' A local church is a motley group of saved sinners who, delivered from sin's power and punishment through Christ's perfect life, atoning death, and glorious resurrection, identify themselves together as his people. They are imperfect, tempted, struggling, sincere, yet growing in the grace and knowledge of Jesus Christ and being conformed day by day to his image. Their new relationship with God in Christ is expressed in their spiritual worship, warfare, and work, as they travel together toward glory and the inheritance of the saints in the light.

This creation of gospel grace in the Lord Jesus is described in various ways. The church is the people of God—a picture of covenantal identity as constituted by the Lord Jesus, comprising the Redeemer and his fellow pilgrims.[1] The church is the kingdom of God—a picture of gracious rule established by Christ her King with the church considered as citizens belonging together in his kingdom.[2] She is the body of Christ—a picture of diversity in unity, given life by her risen Lord, who is the Head, and all the saints as fellow members in that body.[3] She is the temple of God—a picture of divine construction, built by her Saviour, the living stones laid side by side, bound together by the chief Cornerstone.[4] She is the flock of God—a picture of compassionate care, led by Jesus the Good Shepherd and composed of those who together hear his voice and follow him.[5] She is the family of God in a picture of true belonging, in which Jesus as an elder Brother gathers those who will be his Father's adopted children, brothers together.[6] She is the bride of Christ—a picture of sacrificial love, his one bride rejoiced over by Jesus the Bridegroom.[7] She is the garden of God—a picture of

[1] Exod. 6:7; Hos. 2:23; Isa. 43:1 with 1 Pet. 2:9, 10; Titus 2:14; Rev. 21:3, and Eph. 2:11-18.
[2] Mark 1:14, 15; Matt. 12:28: John 18:36; Rom. 14:17; Col. 1:13.
[3] Rom. 12:5 with 1 Cor. 12; Eph. 1:22, 23 cf. Eph.. 5:23; Col. 1:18, 2:19, 3:4; John 15:5.
[4] Matt. 1:23; John 2:19; 4:21-24; 1 Cor. 6:19; 1 Pet. 2:4-6 cf. 1 Cor. 3:16; Eph. 2:20-22.
[5] Psa. 95:6, 7; Heb. 13:20; 1 Pet. 2:25; 5:4.
[6] Heb. 2:10-13, 3:3-6; Rom 9:25, 26 cf. Gal. 3:25; Eph. 1:5.
[7] Isa. 54:5, 62:5, Jer. 2:2; Song of Sol.; Jer 3:1-5; Hos.; Mark 2:18-20; Eph. 5:25; Rom. 5:8; Rev. 19:7-9; 21:2.

nurtured life in which the divine Gardener tends and prunes the branches who have been grafted together into Jesus the Vine, who is the church's life.[8]

The church exists for the praise of the triune God, to whom 'be glory in the church by Christ Jesus, throughout all ages, world without end' (Eph. 3:21). She is called to be holy, having been purchased by the blood of Jesus to this end, each of her members now dead to sin and newly alive to God in Christ Jesus our Lord (Rom. 6:11). The church is animated by that resurrection life that is first in Christ Jesus. Such a status and relationship results in the pursuit of true godliness. This involves on the one hand the deliberate and determined avoidance, rejection and destruction of everything that belongs to the realm of darkness within and without (mortification). On the other hand, it involves the pursuit, cultivation and embrace of all righteousness of body and soul, stirring up all our graces (vivification) in accordance with the divine pattern: 'as he who called you is holy, you also be holy in all your conduct, because it is written, "Be holy, for I am holy"' (1 Pet. 1:15, 16). This process of advancing holiness, called sanctification, is accomplished in dependence upon God, with godly fear: 'Therefore, my beloved, as you have always obeyed, not as in my presence only, but now much more in my absence, work out your own salvation with fear and trembling; for it is God who works in you both to will and to do for his good pleasure' (Phil. 2:12, 13). The people of God are labouring toward the God-appointed and God-secured end of this process, 'for whom [God] foreknew, he also predestined to be conformed to the image of his Son, that he might be the firstborn among many brethren' (Rom. 8:29).

The church of God is governed by her saving and sovereign Lord. John Brown says:

---

[8] Psa. 80:8ff. cf. Isa. 5:1-7; Mark 12:1-12; Luke 13:6-9; John 15:1-8.

A Christian church is a very free society; but they mistake the matter who consider it as a democracy. It is a monarchy, administered by inferior magistrates, chosen by their fellow subjects, who are to execute the King's laws, being guided solely by his word, and neither by their own judgment or caprice, nor by the opinion and will of those whom they govern. Christ is the Lord, and he administers his government by officers appointed according to his ordinance, and regulated by his laws. It is of great importance, both to the office-bearers and private members of a Christian church, that they have distinct scriptural views on this subject, that the former may not exact what they have no right to, and that the latter may not refuse what, by the law of Christ, they are bound to give.[9]

Christ is the crowned and sovereign Head of the body. He exercises and administers his government through those under-shepherds whom he appoints and equips, recognised by 'their fellow subjects' as Christ's gift to the church for her care and protection. The authority of the elders is thus a delegated authority. It derives from a recognised relationship to an acknowledged King, and works out in service to him and to his church. Under such care, the bond of mutual love to Christ and to one another shows itself in various ways, one's attachment to Christ and to his people becoming the primary and governing relationship in all of life.

It is hard to imagine that the triune God would form such a people for his praise and then leave them without direction as to their character and conduct. And we would be right to seek in our Bibles for answers to questions concerning the rule of Christ's church and the manner in which she is to behave herself in the world.

This brings us to the question of church discipline. What is your reaction to that phrase? Does it immediately seem something fearful, something ugly, something alien? Is it something, in short,

[9] John Brown, *1 Peter* (Edinburgh: Banner of Truth Trust, 1975), 2:475-76.

to be shunned if at all possible, left in the dark corners and distant attics of church life?

Robert Murray M'Cheyne struggled with just such a sense when he first became a pastor. He later gave this public testimony:

> When I first entered upon the work of the ministry among you, I was exceedingly ignorant of the vast importance of church discipline. I thought that my great and almost only work was to pray and preach. I saw your souls to be so precious, and the time so short, that I devoted all my time, and care, and strength, to labour in word and doctrine. When cases of discipline were brought before me and the elders, I regarded them with something like abhorrence. It was a duty I shrank from; and I may truly say it nearly drove me from the work of the ministry among you altogether. But it pleased God, who teaches his servants in another way than man teaches, to bless some of the cases of discipline to the manifest and undeniable conversion of the souls of those under our care; and from that hour a new light broke in upon my mind, and I saw that if preaching be an ordinance of Christ, so is church discipline. I now feel very deeply persuaded that both are of God—the two keys are committed to us by Christ: the one the key of doctrine, by means of which we unlock the treasures of the Bible; the other the key of discipline, by which we open or shut the way to the sealing ordinances of the faith. Both are Christ's gift, and neither is to be resigned without sin.[10]

Article XXIX of the Belgic Confession of 1561 gives classic expression to the conviction of the Reformed churches that biblical church discipline is one of the distinguishing marks of a true church of Jesus Christ:

---

[10] Andrew Bonar, *Memoir & Remains of Robert Murray M'Cheyne* (London: Banner of Truth Trust, 1966), 73.

The marks by which the true church is known are these: If the pure doctrine of the gospel is preached therein; if it maintains the pure administration of the sacraments as instituted by Christ; if church discipline is exercised in punishing of sin; in short, if all things are managed according to the pure word of God, all things contrary thereto rejected, and Jesus Christ acknowledged as the only head of the church. Hereby the true church may certainly be known, from which no man has a right to separate himself.[11]

Of course, the apostles got there first. They embraced the founding principles of our Lord himself in the establishment of his congregations, and the relationships within them, with regard to the character of the saints and their mutual pursuit of holiness. The Baptist theologian John Ledley Dagg went so far as to record the suggestion 'that when discipline leaves a church, Christ goes with it.'[12]

We need to consider church discipline carefully. When we understand Christ's teaching on church discipline accurately and scripturally, when we grasp when and how discipline of all kinds should be used, it prevents the kind of abuses that too often crop up in and mar the lives of churches and Christians. When churches and church officers know what means Christ has provided for the health and holiness of his church, it serves to secure the right use of those means. It should prohibit and expose their misuse or abuse. It should prevent pathetic, or pragmatic, or draconian measures being foolishly or wickedly employed. It is for this reason that I am not dealing directly with confusion, errors, or sins in this sphere. When

[11] *Reformed Confessions of the 16th and 17th Centuries in English Translation: Volume 2 (1552–1566),* comp. James T. Dennison, Jr. (Grand Rapids, MI: Reformation Heritage Books, 2010), 442.

[12] J. L. Dagg, *A Treatise on Church Order,* published as *Manual of Church Order* (Harrisonburg, VA: Gano Books, 1990), 274.

it comes to this matter, churches have typically been wrecked and individuals scarred not by faithful and righteous church discipline, but by failures and follies. Injustice and unrighteousness, indiscipline and ill-discipline, whether ignorantly or maliciously, in churches as a whole, or in their officers and members, have produced fearful outcomes. Some faithful churches or church officers face unjust accusations from wilful, disgruntled or ignorant members. Some faithful members suffer unjust dealings at the hands of arrogant officers or clumsy congregations. By setting out what ought to be, I want to provide an antidote to such confusions, tensions and divisions. The misuse and abuse of God's good gifts and righteous principles should never lead to us abandoning what is good and righteous in the first place. Rather, it should send us back to use what is good and righteous in the way and to the end that God intended.

It may be that, having considered all this, our first step in the righteous pursuit of church discipline might be confession of failure or of sin in this sphere of church life. Perhaps there needs to be individual or corporate repentance, the seeking and extending of forgiveness, the restoration of broken relationships.

With these things in mind, let us turn to the topic of church discipline. Building upon these realities, we must consider the Lord's provision for holiness in his house.

The assumptions of discipline

The assumptions of church discipline are rooted in the nature, identity and purpose of the church, as sketched out above. The church is a body called out of the world by God, to God, for God. She is a discernible and distinctive entity to which a person either belongs or does not belong. An individual's attachment to what is often called the universal church is manifest by that individual's commitment to and presence in the local church. The distinctiveness of God's church is, at root, a matter of godliness.

The church has a corporate responsibility to pursue and to manifest that holiness which is pleasing to God and which sets her apart from the world (1 Cor. 5:9, 10; 2 Cor. 6:11–7:1):

> Do not be unequally yoked together with unbelievers. For what fellowship has righteousness with lawlessness? And what communion has light with darkness? And what accord has Christ with Belial? Or what part has a believer with an unbeliever? And what agreement has the temple of God with idols? For you are the temple of the living God. As God has said: 'I will dwell in them and walk among them. I will be their God, and they shall be my people.' Therefore, 'Come out from among them and be separate, says the Lord. Do not touch what is unclean, and I will receive you. I will be a Father to you, and you shall be my sons and daughters, says the Lord Almighty' (2 Cor. 6:14-18)

The church has a recognisable pattern of conduct: 'I write so that you may know how you ought to conduct yourself in the house of God, which is the church of the living God, the pillar and ground of the truth' (1 Tim. 3:15). To the church, sin and holiness do matter and must matter. The people of God are not to think, speak, act or appear like the world through which they are travelling, but rather to show themselves 'blameless and harmless, children of God without fault in the midst of a crooked and perverse generation, among whom you shine as lights in the world' (Phil. 2:15). The church is a creature of distinctive purity. This purity must be cultivated, displayed, maintained and protected. In this purity the privileges, duties, opportunities, liabilities and responsibilities of her members all coalesce and cohere. That distinctive and discernible character is the result of discipline.

The nature of discipline

Church discipline, to many, is—or sounds as if it must be—an unremittingly dark and negative thing. That is to make a grave mistake. Discipline in an army, for example, does not consist solely of reprimands, detentions and courts-martial. The discipline of a school does not consist solely of punishments, demerits and detentions. The discipline of a family does not consist solely in being sent to one's room or degrees of spanking. To imagine such would be to imagine a nonsense. Means are provided for breaches of discipline in all such environments, but the main, regular exercise of discipline is substantially a positive thing. The army is a unit honed into fighting efficiency by training, instruction and correction. The school is formed into an entity by regulation and mutual endeavour in pursuit of common goals. The family is a unit the character and behaviour of which is established by hours of patient investment in a variety of spheres and circumstances. It is similar with Christ's church, in which there are two elements of discipline.

The first is called *formative* or *regulative discipline*. This is the process by which the saints of God invest in one another, under God, individually and corporately. It has in view the eradication of sin and the cultivation of holiness. It is the natural expression of loving fellowship, involving training, instruction and correction. In one sense, every church member is always under discipline. Each member is exhorted to 'warn those who are unruly, comfort the fainthearted, uphold the weak, be patient with all' (1 Thess. 5:14). You are under discipline when you

- exhort one another (Heb. 3:13),
- stir one another up to love and good works (Heb. 10:24),
- love one another (Rom. 13:8),
- receive one another (Rom. 15:7),
- admonish one another (Rom. 15:14),
- care for one another (1 Cor. 12:25),
- serve one another (Gal. 5:13),
- bear with one another (Eph. 4:2),

- forgive one another (Eph. 4:32),
- sing to one another (Eph. 5:19),
- pray for one another (Eph. 6:18),
- comfort one another (1 Thess. 4:18),
- edify one another (1 Thess. 5:11),
- confess sins to one another (James 5:16),
- have compassion for one another (1 Pet. 3:8),
- are hospitable to one another (1 Pet. 4:9),
- minister to one another (1 Pet. 4:10), and
- are submissive to one another (1 Pet. 5:5).

This mutual investment promotes the faith, righteousness, and unity of the church as she pursues holiness in the fear of the Lord.

The second element of discipline is called *corrective* or *restorative discipline*. As we have noted, there are occasions when there are breaches of discipline. There are times when an individual acts against or apart from the body as a whole, compromising its nature and identity, threatening its peace, betraying its doctrine and neglecting its practice. The army cannot afford to overlook the traitor in the ranks. The school cannot afford to ignore the rebel in its midst. The family cannot afford to neglect the disruption of its order. Neither can the church afford to overlook those thoughts, words and deeds which militate against its God-established, God-honouring holiness of character and conduct. Rather, the church, when faced with such conflict and crisis, must act for the protection and preservation of what is good and for the restoration of the offender, preventing damage to the body and pursuing and restoring the health of every one of its members. Because this is more sensitive and contentious, it is here that most difficulties arise. In the words of one wise pastor, 'Everyone believes in church discipline until they have to do it.'

Formative or regulative discipline sets out to form disciples, and righteously to inform and regulate their character and conduct.

Corrective or restorative discipline sets out to correct sinful aberrations among those called disciples, and to restore wandering sheep to the flock.

It is worth noting here that church discipline cannot simply be assumed in the life of the church of Christ. These must be deliberate and definite acts, and they should be planned and purposefully pursued. Formative discipline will not simply happen. It cannot be mechanically produced. As the gardener tends his patch in order to remove the weeds and bring forth fruits and flowers, so the organism that is the church requires tending, nurturing and pruning if she is to produce fruit.

In the same way, it would be a profound mistake to wait until corrective or restorative discipline is required to work out how to proceed in accordance with God's revelation. A crisis is no occasion to work out how to deal with that crisis! The healthy church with wise and caring pastors will work out in times of peace how they will respond, and what processes and patterns they will adopt and follow, should a crisis come. These processes might lie happily fallow for months or years, but they are in place when needed. Corrective discipline is almost invariably a complex and sometimes a messy business. Relationships and reactions, ignorance and uncertainty, together with sin in all parties, can cloud the issues. The clearest principles need to be wisely applied, sometimes under difficult circumstances. However, if a church has understood and embraced those principles of corrective or restorative discipline before they are needed, it will save countless hours and grievous confusion and profound heartaches when those principles are needed.

The motive for discipline

Before we come to the mechanics of discipline, we must consider the motive for it. The motive for church discipline is simply this: *love*. This surprises some people. One of the charges so often brought against a faithful church acting in accordance with Christ's command with regard to discipline—especially restorative—is that the church is unloving. This is simply not the case! To neglect holiness and ignore sin is the most unloving thing we can do. Love does not despise or prevent discipline, it rather guides and directs it: love for God the Father, for his glorious Son, and for his gracious Spirit; love for his church, which is the apple of his eye; and, love for the offender, who is endangering his soul's health. It is love that prompts necessary discipline. In Hebrews 12:6-8, we are told that 'whom the Lord loves he chastens, and scourges every son whom he receives. If you endure chastening, God deals with you as with sons; for what son is there whom a father does not chasten? But if you are without chastening, of which all have become partakers, then you are illegitimate and not sons.' In other words, the absence of discipline reveals the absence of love itself, the absence of belonging, of relationship.

If you love false peace, lazy ease, and a life of uninterrupted pleasure more than you love God and the souls of men, then you will indeed neglect discipline. Love for God and for men demands righteous action when it is necessary. Is it unloving to discipline the soldier who abandons his platoon in battle or betrays them to the enemy?[13] Is it unloving to cast out a traitor from the ranks? Is it unloving to chase off or shoot the wolf which is destroying the sheep? Is it unloving to restrain the man who is walking unawares toward a cliff? Is it unloving to reprimand a child about to plunge its hand into boiling water?

Love lies at the root of formative discipline:

> And now I plead with you, lady, not as though I wrote a new commandment to you, but that which we have had from the beginning: that we love one another. This is love, that we walk

---

[13] Note that the form of discipline will depend on the nature of the offence.

according to his commandments. This is the commandment, that as you have heard from the beginning, you should walk in it (2 John 5, 6).

However, love also drives even the most drastic expressions of corrective discipline. It always aims 'that [a person's] spirit may be saved in the day of the Lord Jesus' (1 Cor. 5:5), just as it produces the tears which flow when such discipline is necessary, carried out in a 'spirit of of gentleness, considering yourself lest you also be tempted' (Gal. 6:1).

The purpose of discipline

Why, then, do we pursue this formative discipline? Why, when necessary, do we pursue restorative discipline? What ends are in sight when we employ these means? We can give at least five answers to that question.

First, we pursue church discipline *to protect the honour of Christ and of his church*. The behaviour, state and character of God's people reflect upon God himself. When Daniel prayed to the Lord, he pleaded with him on the basis that 'your city and your people are called by your name' (Dan. 9:19). The neglecting of holiness and the committing of sin brings dishonour to the God who saves us. This is because the world traces a path back from the character, conduct and concerns of God's people to the character, conduct and concerns of God himself. So David's sin with Bathsheba gave 'great occasion to the enemies of the Lord to blaspheme' (2 Sam. 12:14, compare Rom. 2:24). Paul is horrified when 'brother goes to law against brother, and that before unbelievers' (1 Cor. 6:6), especially when sins are committed in the church that are not even named among the Gentiles (1 Cor. 5:1). Likewise, holiness cultivated and sin mortified displays the purposes of Christ to 'present [the church] to himself a glorious church, not having spot or wrinkle or any such thing, but that she should be holy and without blemish' (Eph. 5:27). Such holiness brings glory to God (1 Pet. 2:12). Men will form their perceptions of you by your actions. They will form their perceptions of Christ as the Head of the church from the actions of the members of his body. If we are concerned for Christ's honour and the honour of his church, we will exercise church discipline.

Secondly, we engage in church discipline *to promote the health and purity of the church.* The church is a body and sickness in one part affects the whole. You would not allow a festering wound in your foot to go untreated because it was 'just a foot.' The effects, the pain, the disturbance, the poison, would work through and disrupt and weaken the whole system. So with sin in the church:

> Your glorying is not good. Do you not know that a little leaven leavens the whole lump? Therefore purge out the old leaven, that you may be a new lump, since you truly are unleavened. For indeed Christ, our Passover, was sacrificed for us. Therefore let us keep the feast, not with old leaven, nor with the leaven of malice and wickedness, but with the unleavened bread of sincerity and truth (1 Cor. 5:6-8).

The church as an outpost of heaven is not a home for ungodliness or a refuge for sin: all such belongs 'outside' (Rev. 22:15). Sin must be purged out of the church lest God himself act in holy judgment and righteous chastisement. Consider that in Corinth the abuses of the Lord's supper was the reason why many were weak and sick among them, and many slept (1 Cor. 11:30). The risen Christ held certain things against those churches that were tolerating wickedness within, and intended to deal with it (Rev. 2:14-25). So we cultivate holiness and address unholiness in the pursuit of healthy and purity.

Thirdly, we undertake church discipline *to punish and plead with those rebelling and wandering.* Chastening is painful and is meant to be (in proper degree and proportion), causing deep sorrow (1 Cor.

5:5). Paul expects the sting of corrective discipline to be such that there could arise a danger of the person disciplined being 'swallowed up with too much sorrow.' The apostle therefore warns the church in Corinth against an unkind harshness, emphasising that the 'punishment[14] which was inflicted by the majority is sufficient for such a man.' Under such circumstances, where there is evidence of repentance, the church should be read to 'forgive and comfort' the offender (2 Cor. 2:5-7), which we shall go on to consider. So you see that corrective discipline exposes the rebel and teaches him his error (1 Tim. 1:20). And yet it is not vindictive—never that! The goal of discipline is not to crush but to stop and reverse the downward slide. From its first actings (Matt. 18:15) to its last words (Gal. 6:1; James 5:19, 20), discipline is a cry to repent, return and be restored. It calls on the wanderer to turn from sin, to seek and receive forgiveness, to return to health, holiness and happiness in communion with God and with his people.

Fourthly, we pursue church discipline *to prevent others from falling into sin*. Discipline makes saints tremble. It builds another barrier against sin. It makes us alert to the presence of sin, teaching us to look 'carefully lest anyone fall short of the grace of God' (Heb. 12:15). It calls us to humility and watchfulness: 'let him who thinks he stands take heed lest he fall' (1 Cor. 10:12). It provokes proper shame and sorrow, stopping us being 'puffed up' and making us mourn (1 Cor. 5:2). It acts as a powerful deterrent, because when sin is publicly rebuked, others fear (1 Tim. 5:20). Even the very act of discipline itself is tempered by the awareness of our own vulnerability: 'Brethren, if a man is overtaken in any trespass, you who are spiritual restore such a one in a spirit of gentleness, considering yourself lest you also be tempted' (Gal. 6:1).

---

[14] The language here refers to a public and formal rebuke or act of censure on the part of the whole congregation.

Fifthly, church discipline is enacted *to provide a witness to the world*. It tells the world—or, it should tell the world (1 Cor. 5:1)—that holiness matters and that sin is not to be taken lightly, either within or without the professing church. The way in which the church pursues holiness (Matt. 5:16; John 13:34, 35; 2 Cor. 6:14-71; 1 Pet. 2:12) and purges sin (1 Cor. 5:2, 6, 7) is a potent testimony to the watching world of the character of God and of the judgment to come:

> Therefore, since all these things will be dissolved, what manner of persons ought you to be in holy conduct and godliness, looking for and hastening the coming of the day of God, because of which the heavens will be dissolved, being on fire, and the elements will melt with fervent heat? Nevertheless we, according to his promise, look for new heavens and a new earth in which righteousness dwells. Therefore, beloved, looking forward to these things, be diligent to be found by him in peace, without spot and blameless (2 Pet. 3:11-14).

Sixthly, church discipline aims *to please the Head of the church and so preserve the power of the gospel*. What will happen in a church that neglects the pursuit of holiness and indulges sin in its midst? Will that church know God's smile? We cannot anticipate that the Lord will own the preaching of men who have no regard for the purity of Christ's bride. We cannot anticipate that the God of heaven will manifest his favour to a congregation that despises his commands, except first, in mercy, calling them back to a more righteous way. If we want the witness of the church to be effective and the preaching of the gospel to be credible, we cannot turn a blind eye to sin in our midst.

It is love—love for God, for one another, for the offender, for our own souls, and for the world—which drives us in our pursuit of godliness and our resistance to sin. Men may hate believers for their holiness, just as 'Herodias held it against [John] and wanted to kill him, but could not' (Mark 6:19). By the same token, our credibility and potency with men hang upon our holiness, just as 'Herod feared John, knowing that he was a just and holy man, and protected him. And when he heard him, he did many things, and heard him gladly' (Mark 6:20 cf. 1 Pet. 4:4).

The reasons for discipline

The church should be a group of saints cheerfully and diligently pursuing spiritual wholeness and true holiness in our faith and life together. We are a community of disciples, those who follow and learn from Jesus Christ as Lord. We acknowledge that this is not an easy pattern of life to maintain. We therefore need formative or regulative discipline, by which we assist, enable, encourage, and exhort one another in the pursuit and attainment of the legitimate, biblical standards of godliness. But it is too easy to stumble, even to abandon—albeit temporarily—such a pursuit. Therefore we also need corrective or restorative discipline as a means of stopping us short and bringing us back when necessary. In brief, sins of omission or commission carried out without repentance are the occasions of or reasons for discipline. The risk or reality of leaving undone something that must be done, or of doing what must not be done, calls forth the discipline of the church in some way. Albert Mohler helpfully identifies three spheres in which the church must keep up her guard.[15]

Firstly, the church must maintain and guard *fidelity of doctrine*. Paul warned the Ephesian elders about 'savage wolves' who would not spare the flock, but—rising up from among the elders them-

[15] http://www.the-highway.com/discipline_Mohler.html, accessed 25th August 2011. This article is a chapter from *The Compromised Church: The Present Evangelical Crisis*, ed. John H. Armstrong (Wheaton, IL: Crossway Books, 1998). The next three headings are adopted from Mohler's chapter.

selves—would speak 'perverse things, to draw away the disciples after themselves' (Acts 20:29, 30). One of the abiding concerns of the apostles and their co-labourers was the danger posed by false teachers. Paul's language is uncompromising:

> But even if we, or an angel from heaven, preach any other gospel to you than what we have preached to you, let him be accursed. As we have said before, so now I say again, if anyone preaches any other gospel to you than what you have received, let him be accursed (Gal. 1:8, 9).

Peter and Jude paint equally and unremittingly bleak pictures of such men:

> But there were also false prophets among the people, even as there will be false teachers among you, who will secretly bring in destructive heresies, even denying the Lord who bought them, and bring on themselves swift destruction (2 Pet. 2:1).

> For certain men have crept in unnoticed, who long ago were marked out for this condemnation, ungodly men, who turn the grace of our God into lewdness and deny the only Lord God and our Lord Jesus Christ (Jude 4).

Such false teachers are to be identified, individually and personally, and in connection with their heretical doctrine. They must be exposed, avoided and cast out—both their teaching and their persons rejected. Paul points out such men without hesitation to Timothy, urging him to have 'faith and a good conscience, which some having rejected, concerning the faith have suffered shipwreck, of whom are Hymenaeus and Alexander, whom I delivered to Satan that they may learn not to blaspheme' (1 Tim. 1:19, 20). Later, Paul gives a general description of such false teachers, and an equally blunt response to them:

> If anyone teaches otherwise and does not consent to wholesome

words, even the words of our Lord Jesus Christ, and to the doctrine which accords with godliness, he is proud, knowing nothing, but is obsessed with disputes and arguments over words, from which come envy, strife, reviling, evil suspicions, useless wranglings of men of corrupt minds and destitute of the truth, who suppose that godliness is a means of gain. From such withdraw yourself (1 Tim. 6:3-5).

The apostle John, one of the 'sons of thunder,' beloved of Christ, also quite rightly hurls his lightning against such men:

Whoever transgresses and does not abide in the doctrine of Christ does not have God. He who abides in the doctrine of Christ has both the Father and the Son. If anyone comes to you and does not bring this doctrine, do not receive him into your house nor greet him; for he who greets him shares in his evil deeds (2 John 9-11).

Concerning another passage from the same apostle, Calvin encourages us that there are certain things we should always bear in mind when we hear what John wrote concerning spiritual seducers:

it is the duty of a good and diligent pastor not only to gather a flock, but also to drive away wolves: for what will it avail to proclaim the pure gospel, if we connive at the impostures of Satan? No one, then, can faithfully teach the church, except he is diligent in banishing errors whenever he finds them spread by seducers.[16]

If the gospel is perverted, then God is assaulted, Christ is veiled, righteousness is endangered, and the world is undone. Church discipline must be concerned with fidelity of doctrine; confusion and compromise are too costly to be ignored.

[16] John Calvin, *Commentaries* (Calvin Translation Society, 1855), comments on 1 John 2:26.

Secondly, the church must maintain and guard *purity of life*. The church is called to comprehensive and consistent holiness. The Lord her God is unashamed to establish a high moral-ethical standard for every sphere of life.[17] Christians are being conformed to the image of the holy Son of God. The church therefore ought to be marked by the absence of those sins characteristic of unconverted men and women—the things we once were (1 Cor. 6:9-11)—and rebellion against God and his established order (2 Thess. 3:6-15). The church ought to be a God-honouringly and distinctively pure body in a filthy environment:

> Therefore 'Come out from among them and be separate, says the Lord. Do not touch what is unclean, and I will receive you. I will be a Father to you, and you shall be my sons and daughters, says the LORD Almighty.' Therefore, having these promises, beloved, let us cleanse ourselves from all filthiness of the flesh and spirit, perfecting holiness in the fear of God (2 Cor. 6:17–7:1 compare Phil 2:15; 1 Pet. 2:11, 12; 4:15, 16).

Sin cripples the church and besmirches her Saviour in the eyes of men. Sin leaves the bride of Christ drowning in the very filth out of which she ought to be pulling those in need of saving. An unholy Christian is a contradiction in terms, and anyone not living as a Christian is not entitled to the name or the privileges of a Christian. Take a look at the social networking efforts of some who name the name of Christ and you will quickly find many whose interests, language and activities are indistinguishable from the openly ungodly. These things ought not to be. They certainly ought not to be accepted in the church. Church discipline must be concerned with purity of life; carnality and ungodliness cannot be overlooked.

[17] We need only turn to such passages as Matthew 15:19, 20, Romans 13:8-14, Ephesians 4:25–6:8, Colossians 3:5–4:6, 1 Thessalonians 4:1-10, 2 Timothy 3:22–4:5, Titus 1:16, 2:1–3:3, and so on and so forth, to determine the truth of that statement.

Thirdly, the church must maintain and guard *unity of fellowship*. The bond of love is a primary and distinctive feature of the church: 'A new commandment I give to you, that you love one another; as I have loved you, that you also love one another. By this all will know that you are my disciples, if you have love for one another' (John 13:34, 35). Unity is a mark by which the true church is, or ought to be, identifiable. We should not be surprised, then, that unholy division and schism are to be resisted at all costs:

> 'With the tongue we bless our God and Father, and with it we curse men, who have been made in the similitude of God. Out of the same mouth proceed blessing and cursing. My brethren, these things ought not to be so' (James 3:9, 10; compare Gal. 5:13-15).

Words and deeds which divide, disrupt and destroy the church are not to be tolerated. Paul urges the Roman Christians to

> note those who cause divisions and offences, contrary to the doctrine which you learned, and avoid them. For those who are such do not serve our Lord Jesus Christ, but their own belly, and by smooth words and flattering speech deceive the hearts of the simple' (Rom. 16:17, 18).

To Titus he writes, 'reject a divisive man after the first and second admonition, knowing that such a person is warped and sinning, being self-condemned' (Titus 3:10, 11). The spirit which divides a church into factions following merely human figureheads, thus causing contention, is to be avoided at all costs (1 Cor. 1:10-13). That attractive 'unity of the Spirit in the bond of peace' is to be pursued (Eph. 4:3). Therefore, offences are to be swiftly resolved (Matt. 5:23, 24), not least because divisions make a mockery of the Lord's supper (1 Cor. 11:26-29). To abandon or assault the body of Christ is serious business. That is why private offences must be dealt with, non-attendance addressed, and the table of the Lord guarded.

Discipline itself is not divisive when righteously practised and embraced by the church. It is actually a primary means of securing and maintaining true unity. Church discipline must be concerned with unity of fellowship; disruption and divisiveness are no small offence in the eyes of the living God.

The practice of discipline

So how is this discipline to be carried out? Fundamentally, it is—in one way or another—a constant feature of church life. Formative discipline is the ongoing impress of the word of God in and by the preaching and teaching, worked out and pressed home in the fellowship of the saints. When there are aberrations that break out in the faith and life of the professing people of God, the Lord has—in his infinite wisdom and mercy—provided a sequence of steps to put a stop to sin, restore relationships, and reset the pursuit of holiness.

Generally speaking, corrective or restorative discipline takes place at the same level at which the breach of formative or regulative discipline occurs. That is, a private, personal offence generally requires a private, personal rebuke, with private, personal repentance, reconciliation and restoration. Public offences require a public response.

Perhaps the simplest outline of corrective discipline found in Scripture is Matthew 18:15-20:

> Moreover if your brother sins against you, go and tell him his fault between you and him alone. If he hears you, you have gained your brother. But if he will not hear, take with you one or two more, that 'by the mouth of two or three witnesses every word may be established.' And if he refuses to hear them, tell it to the church. But if he refuses even to hear the church, let him be to you like a heathen and a tax collector. Assuredly, I say to you, whatever you bind on earth will be bound in heaven, and

whatever you loose on earth will be loosed in heaven. Again I say to you that if two of you agree on earth concerning anything that they ask, it will be done for them by my Father in heaven. For where two or three are gathered together in my name, I am there in the midst of them.

Here is the promise of Christ's spiritual presence with his people as they conduct their business as a church. Again, if Christ takes the holiness of his people so seriously, how serious ought to be our response to sin?

The simple trajectory of these verses again assumes a context in which formative discipline is taking place as a matter of course. This is a healthy environment of mutual and appropriate regard and concern for the health of my own soul and the souls of my brothers and sisters. However, in the sequence which Christ envisions, there is an instance of sin within the body. That sin has been righteously addressed but there has been no righteous response. That is, it is a matter in which the blanket of love can no longer be drawn over the offence. The fervent love which covers a multitude of sins (1 Pet. 4:8)—the love which 'suffers long and is kind … does not envy … does not parade itself, is not puffed up; does not behave rudely, does not seek its own, is not provoked, thinks no evil; does not rejoice in iniquity, but rejoices in the truth; bears all things, believes all things, hopes all things, endures all things' (1 Cor. 13:4-7)—must now take prayerful account of the realities of the case. Love must step out in the painful but necessary step of a gracious confrontation. There is no stewing over the matter, brooding unhealthily upon it, creating a distance between the offender and the offended. There is no complaining or gossip, repeating a matter and separating friends (Prov. 17:9).

Let us assume—in love!—that the offended brother approaches the offending brother in this spirit of love. He speaks graciously and honestly and tenderly. He levels no unreasonable accusations. The offended brother explains his reasons for so coming in a way that reveals no animosity or personal grudge. He takes pains to impute nothing, but to judge righteously. For sure, there are few if any who can so speak such things as to give no grounds of needless offence. However, in a healthy relationship the one who comes in such a spirit ought to be received in the same spirit. Spurgeon's counsel is wise: 'We must seek out the offender, and tell him his fault as if he were not aware of it; as perhaps he may not be.'[18] The speaker avoids the typical pitfalls: 'You always ...' and, 'You never ...' He steers clear of other such traps, and in a spirit of humility and tenderness identifies the particular sin of which he fears the offender may be guilty. It is a private transaction. You 'tell him his fault between you and him alone,' not in a spirit of vindictiveness but with a disposition to forgive. (How we wish all church members showed such a spirit at all times!)

How will the offender respond? It may be that he has a legitimate and righteous explanation which demonstrates that the charge is unfounded. For example, the offended brother may, with the best of intentions, have misconstrued some word or event. They just got hold of the wrong end of the stick! Thankfully, all can quickly be set straight. If so, the offended party should quickly and readily let go of his concern without further brooding. He or she should not embark on a witch hunt, though he may reasonably be aware of the pattern or occasion which first sparked that concern in future dealings with the friend to whom he speaks. The one who was considered an offender should not hold a grudge against the one who comes to him, or use the opportunity for a little tit-for-tat, but should appreciate the love which acted with such generous boldness.

Or, it may be that there is a matter of sin which has been accurately identified. In this instance, there are basically only two

---

[18] C. H. Spurgeon, *Commentary on Matthew: The Gospel of the Kingdom* (Edinburgh: Banner of Truth Trust, 2010), 260.

along with my spirit, with the power of our Lord Jesus Christ, deliver such a one to Satan for the destruction of the flesh, that his spirit may be saved in the day of the Lord Jesus.

Here the public and gross nature of the sin demands an immediate and significant act of the gathered church to identify this behaviour as that which puts the impenitent transgressor outside the holy community. This is an act in which Paul has a definite and authoritative interest, but one in which the apostle acts with and alongside rather than apart from or over the church.

Now, we may see that relatively simple process and say, 'But it is never that straightforward!' It is sadly true that it is rarely so simple and clean as this. Sometimes a sin—as in the Corinthian church—is immediately general and public rather than personal and private, and it ought to be addressed accordingly. Sometimes sin is subtle and complex rather than open and simple. Sin can be hidden behind a tissue of deceit or disguised within a web of evasions and avoidances and denials. That is why the church as a whole and the elders in particular are given, in other parts of the New Testament, additional and supplementary principles, counsels and means by which church discipline may be righteously carried out with a view to the repentance and restoration of the offender. So, for example, there is Romans 16:17, 18:

> Now I urge you, brethren, note those who cause divisions and offences, contrary to the doctrine which you learned, and avoid them. For those who are such do not serve our Lord Jesus Christ, but their own belly, and by smooth words and flattering speech deceive the hearts of the simple.

Here the brothers are to note divisive people—those who deliberately and unrepentantly disrupt the unity of the body of Christ by their words and deeds—and they are to avoid them. The church is to turn away from such, having nothing to do with them. It may be that this divisive spirit is first recognised at an individual level, or it may be something that the elders note in their shepherding of the flock and bring before the church.

In 2 Thessalonians 3:6-15, there is a series of injunctions to the church:

> But we command you, brethren, in the name of our Lord Jesus Christ, that you withdraw from every brother who walks disorderly and not according to the tradition which he received from us. For you yourselves know how you ought to follow us, for we were not disorderly among you; nor did we eat anyone's bread free of charge, but worked with labour and toil night and day, that we might not be a burden to any of you, not because we do not have authority, but to make ourselves an example of how you should follow us. For even when we were with you, we commanded you this: If anyone will not work, neither shall he eat. For we hear that there are some who walk among you in a disorderly manner, not working at all, but are busybodies. Now those who are such we command and exhort through our Lord Jesus Christ that they work in quietness and eat their own bread. But as for you, brethren, do not grow weary in doing good. And if anyone does not obey our word in this epistle, note that person and do not keep company with him, that he may be ashamed. Yet do not count him as an enemy, but admonish him as a brother.

Here Paul commands a withdrawing from the 'disorderly': these are the ones who behave irresponsibly with regard to God's commands and principles of righteousness and justice. In context, these are people who show that they have no regard for God's creation ordinance of labour. More broadly, they seem ready to reject some of the most basic principles of righteous responsibility before God and men. The church is to keep away from them with a view to their being brought to shame. Nevertheless, in this instance the sinner is not to be counted as an enemy, but admonished as a brother. A distinction is made with regard to his standing in relation to the church. There is a degree of drawing back within the body but not a putting out from the body. There is a further option here for the church in seeking to bring the wanderer back to a pattern of righteous conviction and behaviour.

Again, there is 1 Timothy 5:19, 20: 'Do not receive an accusation against an elder except from two or three witnesses. Those who are sinning rebuke in the presence of all, that the rest also may fear.' The pastors of a church are not immune to or above discipline, but may be particularly vulnerable to false charges. As men whose character has been previously assessed and is constantly on display and monitored, they are entitled to an additional degree of credit. However, they are also liable to a particular degree of shame if they dishonour their Master and his calling. If there is sin, they are to be rebuked 'in the presence of all, that the rest may also fear.' That is, they are either to be openly rebuked in the presence of all the elders, or in the presence of all the church, in order that a healthy degree of godly fear may characterise the church and her pastors. It is a reminder that no gifts or graces put a man outside the reach of sin or the need of believing repentance. (Note also that the elder who will not face the fact of his sin ought to be proceeded against on the same basis as any other member of the church. He faces the loss of his office if his character falls short of the absolute standard that the Lord imposes for holding office, as well as—potentially—his standing as a saint).

Finally, there is Titus 3:10, 11, where the Lord's apostle tells the church to 'reject a divisive man after the first and second admonition, knowing that such a person is warped and sinning, being self-condemned.' Again, divisiveness is the primary concern. Here a divisive person is to be admonished: righteousness and transgression (categories governed by the truth of the word) are to be held before his eyes and ears so as to be imprinted upon his heart. He is to receive clear instruction and warning about his inappropriate words and behaviour. If he rejects such instruction and warning, this leads to his rejection by the church. He is to feel the chill wind caused by the church drawing back from him, so that he knows himself to be outside the spiritual building. Again, there may be a suggestion here that the elders (given their peculiar responsibility and oversight) are to take the lead in such action, although it is not necessarily the elders to whom this responsibility of admonition is restricted.[22]

Peter Ackroyd draws on Martin Bucer to summarise helpfully the balance of role and responsibility within the church, taking into account the various ways and means of accomplishing the appointed ends:

> The discipline of life and manners is a pastoral function, and requires that 'not only the public ministers of the church (though these principally) but even individual Christians should exercise a care for their neighbours. By the authority and magisterium of our Lord Jesus Christ, each person should strengthen and advance his neighbours wherever this is possible, and urge them to progress in the life of God, as his disciples, in his faith and knowledge. And if they fall into error of doctrine or some vice of life or manners, whoever can should with utmost zeal recall such persons from all false doctrine and depraved activity, both for the purity of Christian doctrine and

[22] Further insights might be gleaned by a careful study of instances of sin identified and addressed by God and his people throughout the New Testament Scriptures. These might include Ananias and Sapphira; Simon Magus; Euodia and Syntyche; the immoral Corinthian; the dying Corinthians who offended Christ at his table; the divisive Cretans; the disorderly Thessalonians; the divisive and offensive Romans; Hymenaeus and Alexander; Philetus; perhaps the restoration of Peter; the division between Peter and Paul over the gospel to the Gentiles; the seven churches of Asia Minor. It might also be profitable to consider some of the Old Testament parallels.

the sedulous [diligent and persistent] conformity of all life to the will of God.'

On the basis of Matthew 18, all Christians share responsibility for encouraging both right belief and godly conduct: 'For Christ, our master and governor, lives in each Christian. In each, therefore, and through the ministry of each, he seeks and saves the lost. On this account it is necessary that whoever are really of Christ should have a vigilant care for their brethren on his authority and power and eagerly exhort whomever they can to their duty, and keep all from sins according to their ability or rescue those who have fallen into them.'

The discipline exercised by pastors and elders is supplementary to this mutual ministry of fraternal correction and encouragement among believers. It remains a weighty responsibility: 'Those whom the Lord has put in charge of his sheep should therefore ponder seriously the fact that from their hands will be required whatever sheep perish by their negligence.' Indeed, Bucer calls on the church's ministers to restore the public exercise of excommunication over serious public sin: 'the faithful ministers of Christ should not tolerate in the company of Christ, nor admit to the sacraments of Christ, those whom they cannot and should not acknowledge by their fruits, according to the precepts of the Lord, to be his true disciples and followers.'[23]

Ackroyd, following Bucer, is emphasising that the elders have particular responsibility as part of their oversight to respond righteously to sin. Indeed, their specific duties mean that they 'take point' in this regard, and will often be the first ones to recognise and address particular sins. They are—by their teaching and example—to

[23] Peter Ackroyd, *Strangers to Correction: Christian Discipline and the English Reformation* (St Antholin's Lectureship Charity Lecture, 2003), 6-7. The quotations are from Bucer's *De Regno Christi*.

ensure that the standards of righteousness are maintained and enacted within the church of Jesus Christ.

We might attempt a careful conclusion. All church discipline is a demonstration of love. Formative discipline is the loving employment of the normal means provided by the Lord to keep his church in a holy and healthy condition. Corrective discipline occurs when the church perceives one who is considered a brother on a tragic downward trajectory into unrepentant sin. The church (her individual members, not least her undershepherds, with the whole body acting in concert when required) therefore acts lovingly, wisely and appropriately, using all the scriptural means at her disposal. She employs the basic sequence of Matthew 18:15-20, with a range of other pleas and censures and sanctions available to her. The aim is to prevent the offender's acceleration and escalation along that path of sin. The intention is to bring about the repentance and restoration of the one who is sinning. If the church fails to secure this end, she must make plain by her attitudes and words and deeds—with tenderness and tears—that such patterns of unrepentant sin are not characteristic of the professing Christian and will not be tolerated in the church of the living God.

The sting of discipline

Let us not pretend that discipline is pleasant. It is not. Formative discipline is hard work as we are trained for righteousness against the inclinations of the flesh and the impressions of the world. It is never pleasant to have our frailties and failures pointed out, however tenderly. It requires of us a genuine humility married to an earnest desire for godliness. There must be a readiness to swallow sometimes bitter medicine in the pursuit of spiritual health. Corrective discipline is often unpalatable to those exercising it, as well as painful to those receiving it: 'Now no chastening seems to be joyful for the present, but painful' (Heb. 12:11). William M. Taylor makes very plain how our responses to rebuke show our hearts:

It may seem a paradox to say it, but there are few things which test a man's real Christianity more than reproof for that which is actually blameworthy. It is comparatively easy to guard against giving offence; but it is exceeding hard to keep from taking offence in such circumstances, and to say with the Psalmist, 'Let the righteous smite me; it shall be a kindness: and let him reprove me; it shall be an excellent oil, which shall not break my head.' We all assent to Solomon's proverb, 'Open rebuke is better than secret love'; but when the rebuke comes most of us, on the whole, would prefer the love; and too frequently we are disposed to resent the faithfulness of the brother who would hint, even in the most delicate manner, that we have been in the wrong. We cry out against the modern dogma of papal infallibility, but we have all too much belief in that [dogma] of our own infallibility; for our tempers are roused, and our hearts are estranged by any exposure of our error or inconsistency. How many personal alienations and ecclesiastical schisms might have been prevented, if there had been on the one side the honest frankness of Paul, and on the other the manly meekness of Peter as these come out in this transaction![24]

Again, the assumption that lies behind the exercise of corrective discipline is the nature of commitment to the church of Christ Jesus. In the words of the *1689 (Second London) Baptist Confession of Faith* (chapter 26, paragraph 12): 'As all believers are bound to join themselves to particular churches, when and where they have opportunity so to do; so all that are admitted unto the privileges of a church, are also under the censures and government thereof, according to the rule of Christ.'[25]

[24] William M. Taylor, *Paul the Missionary* (London: Charles Burnet & Co, 1892), 175-76. Almost identical language appears in the author's earlier treatment of *Peter, the Apostle* (London: Charles Burnet & Co, 1891), 300-1.

[25] Similar language is found in the *Savoy Platform of Polity*. The *Westminster Confession of Faith* deals with the matter of church discipline specifically in Chapter 30, 'Of Church

In other words, the privileges, responsibilities, liabilities, duties and opportunities of church fellowship belong and hold together. No one is free simply to stroll up and select all the portions of church life that they like and leave behind those which they find unpalatable. Church life is not a spiritual smorgasbord. The blessings must be embraced, and should only be embraced, alongside the commitments to the body as a whole to sustain true doctrine, discipleship and devotion. Those responsibilities righteously embraced qualify us for the associated privileges. The privileges of church membership are not inalienable Christian rights apart from any Christian commitments. They are the blessings of those who have become accountable to one another for their faith and life once they are both personally and corporately identified as members together of the body of Christ.

Church members are those who can enter into and participate in the life of the church without dishonouring Christ, disgracing the saints, bringing the church into disrepute or bringing condemnation upon themselves. If they fall short of this standard, and continue to do so unrepentantly, the church must act. Church discipline is the chill of frost that reminds them of the privileges and blessings that they forfeit by behaving as if they were no part of the body; it therefore requires that they be treated accordingly. If discipline had no teeth—if the church lacked all scope for effective censure and sanction—then that discipline would be pointless and unprofitable. This is why we need to reckon with its substance. Again, consider some of the passages already identified and a few others besides:

> And if he refuses to hear them, tell it to the church. But if he refuses even to hear the church, let him be to you like a heathen and a tax collector (Matt. 18:17).

Censures.' Similar convictions about the nature of the church underpin all these statements, although Presbyterian polity differs in some of its emphases from Independency. Our primary concern here is with and within the local church.

And you are puffed up, and have not rather mourned, that he who has done this deed might be taken away from among you. … deliver such a one to Satan for the destruction of the flesh, that his spirit may be saved in the day of the Lord Jesus. … I wrote to you in my epistle not to keep company with sexually immoral people. Yet I certainly did not mean with the sexually immoral people of this world, or with the covetous, or extortioners, or idolaters, since then you would need to go out of the world. But now I have written to you not to keep company with anyone named a brother, who is sexually immoral, or covetous, or an idolater, or a reviler, or a drunkard, or an extortioner—not even to eat with such a person (1 Cor. 5:2, 5, 9-11).

… on the contrary, you ought rather to forgive and comfort him [the repentant sinner], lest perhaps such a one be swallowed up with too much sorrow (2 Cor. 2:7).

But we command you, brethren, in the name of our Lord Jesus Christ, that you withdraw from every brother who walks disorderly and not according to the tradition which he received from us. … And if anyone does not obey our word in this epistle, note that person and do not keep company with him, that he may be ashamed. Yet do not count him as an enemy, but admonish him as a brother (2 Thess. 3:6, 14, 15).

This charge I commit to you, son Timothy, according to the prophecies previously made concerning you, that by them you may wage the good warfare, having faith and a good conscience, which some having rejected, concerning the faith have suffered shipwreck, of whom are Hymenaeus and Alexander, whom I delivered to Satan that they may learn not to blaspheme (1 Tim. 1:18-20)

Those who are sinning rebuke in the presence of all, that the rest also may fear (1 Tim. 5:20).

But know this, that in the last days perilous times will come: For men will be lovers of themselves, lovers of money, boasters, proud, blasphemers, disobedient to parents, unthankful, unholy, unloving, unforgiving, slanderers, without self-control, brutal, despisers of good, traitors, headstrong, haughty, lovers of pleasure rather than lovers of God, having a form of godliness but denying its power. And from such people turn away! (2 Tim. 3:1-5).

Reject a divisive man after the first and second admonition, knowing that such a person is warped and sinning, being self-condemned (Titus 3:10, 11).

The fearful judgments of time—and, potentially, of eternity—held out in these verses ought to strike a holy fear into the heart of every Christian whose thinking and feeling is governed by Scripture. The prospect of being put out of the congregation of the righteous as if you have no part in their inheritance, of being delivered over to Satan, of painful admonition, of shameful rebuke, of cutting rejection, of the suspension of the privileges of church membership as one who has dishonoured Christ, soiled his profession or divided the church—how can this not make us humble and careful? Only if we fail lightly to esteem those privileges now!

Again, Bucer says concerning 2 Thessalonians 3:

From this text we realise how much authority has been given to us in order to apply to sinful brethren this remedy of salutary abstention and avoidance and how much the Lord wishes this thing to work in healing the wounds of the brethren. *For those who are not entirely hopeless it is an intolerable torment of mind to be excluded from the company of the brethren and of the whole church, and to be avoided by all, like men profane and alien to Christ our Lord.* When such pressure is used, sinning brethren are moved to repentance and brought back to their duty much more effectively than by other punishments … let us think over how much we harm both the sinning brethren and the entire church when we deprive those brethren who are involved in misdeeds of this medicine of holy severity.[26]

There ought to be no ugly appetite for 'this medicine of holy severity' in a true child of God. A failure to esteem the privileges of the child of God in the family of God, and to fear the associated forfeits, is a terrible mark of the man in rebellion against God and his church, and it causes the true saint much grief, even as the church acts against it.

Let me add a note about the relationships between churches. Faithful gospel churches ought to ensure that they do not undo or despise the actings of other such churches by making their discipline of no effect. What if a person is righteously deprived of some or all of the privileges of membership, and has only to stroll down the road in order to receive them again from unthinking or unprincipled saints in another congregation? Little is more damaging to the souls of men or the communion between saints on the collective level. It is right and appropriate for the elders of one congregation to communicate the status of a member under discipline to other churches. If need be, they should identify part or whole of the circumstances which brought it about. They do this for the safety of other people and for the purity of the church. It is equally to be expected that faithful churches should respect the acts of discipline carried out by other faithful churches, lest the teeth of discipline be drawn and its ends and aims negated.

Corrective or restorative discipline may be a holy grief to those who exercise it, but it is medicine administered for the good of the sinning soul. It is a necessary purgative, required to cause sorrow and

[26] From Martin Bucer's *De Regno Christi*, quoted in Peter Ackroyd, *Strangers to Correction: Christian Discipline and the English Reformation* (St Antholin's Lectureship Charity Lecture, 2003), 8, emphasis added.

shame in order to alert the wanderer to the errors and dangers of his way, and to bring him back, in repentance vomiting the poison of his sin out of his system. The aim is to restore the sinner, through repentance and forgiveness, to spiritual health and to the safety and security of the community of faithful disciples.

The success of discipline

Let us not continue without at least noting the joy when such restoration is accomplished. It is when a sinner repents that the disposition of the one or ones against whom the sin was committed is revealed. We see, then, the heart of God revealed when there is joy in the presence of the angels over one sinner who repents (see Luke 15). It is the same when a son repents and is restored:

> Blessed is he whose transgression is forgiven,
> Whose sin is covered.
> Blessed is the man to whom the LORD does not impute iniquity,
> And in whose spirit there is no deceit.
> When I kept silent, my bones grew old
> Through my groaning all the day long.
> For day and night
> Your hand was heavy upon me;
> My vitality was turned into the drought of summer.
> I acknowledged my sin to You,
> And my iniquity I have not hidden.
> I said, 'I will confess my transgressions to the LORD,'
> And You forgave the iniquity of my sin (Psa. 32:1-5).

This divine readiness to receive, forgive and restore is the model for the children of God: 'be kind to one another, tenderhearted, forgiving one another, just as God in Christ forgave you' (Eph. 4:32).

So our Lord gives instructions to his disciples concerning life in his church. Peter queries the nature and extent of forgiveness, with perhaps the implied question that there must be a limit to this seeming folly of forgiveness. Peter asks 'Lord, how often shall my brother sin against me, and I forgive him? Up to seven times?' Jesus says to him, 'I do not say to you, up to seven times, but up to seventy times seven.' Our Lord goes on to tell the parable of the unforgiving servant, who—having been forgiven his own great debt—refused to deal mercifully with the relatively insignificant debt of those who owed something to him (Matt. 18:21-24).

In the same way, the apostle Paul gives counsel to the Corinthian church. When he writes in rebuke his intention is that he should be made righteously glad by the righteous and repentant sorrow of those with whom he has had to deal in justice, dispensing 'this medicine of holy severity.' He applies the very same principle to the whole church with regard to the punishment inflicted upon the man in their midst who had sinned:

> For out of much affliction and anguish of heart I wrote to you, with many tears, not that you should be grieved, but that you might know the love which I have so abundantly for you. But if anyone has caused grief, he has not grieved me, but all of you to some extent—not to be too severe. This punishment which was inflicted by the majority is sufficient for such a man, so that, on the contrary, you ought rather to forgive and comfort him, lest perhaps such a one be swallowed up with too much sorrow. Therefore I urge you to reaffirm your love to him (2 Cor. 2:4-8).

There is a fearful danger that discipline will or may be abused. As we have said before, church discipline abused typically proves as damaging to Christ's cause as discipline neglected. The discipline righteously enacted in Christian love never sets out merely to crush someone and leave them crushed. It is never to be vindictive (Gal. 6:1) or vengeful (Rom. 12:19). It is not to be aggressive or excessive, carried out in a merciless spirit. It is not a tool for incompetent or abusive under-shepherds to lord it over the flock (Mark 10:42; 1 Pet. 5:1-4). It is never to be a means of building or defending a power base, of fighting factional wars within a congregation by accusation and counter-accusation. It should never become some kind of perverse badge of orthodoxy (all too easily done with a church seeking to reform, or even zealously desiring to make their allegiance to God and their embrace of his holiness known). There are some sad cases of churches which seem to imagine that the more cases of discipline they have to parade or reveal the more holy they must be and are seen to be. Discipline at its best is a sad and sorrowful business, never a matter for boasting.

Let us never forget that abuses of discipline are observed by the God and Father of our Lord Jesus Christ. That same Saviour is the one against whom men act when they act against his true saints. How fearful, then, deliberately to abuse the keys of the kingdom for personal gain or advancement and have to face the judge of all the earth! How fearful, even, to mistakenly bruise or carelessly crush a sorrowing sinner when Christ is ready to bind him up, and desires that the church should act in his name to accomplish these things. How fearful to reject or neglect true and faithful discipline! For such abuses we must answer to God himself, in accordance with whose character we ought always to be acting. The day of judgment will deal not only with those who have evaded discipline or seemed to get away with sin, but will also be a terror to those who have abused discipline as a means of committing sin.

Righteous discipline, then, is to be carried out so that the repentance of the offender might be a source of true gladness to the church welcoming the sinner home. The discipline ought to be appropriate and proportionate. When, God willing, it accomplishes its end and brings the wounded man back to God and his people, he ought to be forgiven and comforted, those wounds bound up and great care taken for his health and wholeness. This is because there is a real danger that the offender who has at last come to himself will be 'swallowed up with too much sorrow.' He may be forgiven by men and by God, but he may struggle to embrace his status as forgiven. He may struggle to reckon himself clean and accepted in Christ with God, and accepted for Christ's sake among his people. There is a danger of dejection and despair, a fear that he will forever be a second-class citizen in the kingdom of heaven. It may lead to further distance and division within the church. Doubtless Satan would love to have it so!

When the offender finally hears his brothers, and is restored through the seeking, extending, and receiving of forgiveness, there must be a conscientious reaffirmation of love. To be sure, care must be taken to assess the sincerity of repentant words, but we can only evaluate the state of a man's heart by what he says and does. Such caution is right and wise, especially when the sin has been long-pursued and become deeply ingrained, or is particularly dangerous for others. Nevertheless, love dictates that we take a penitent confession of sin and a desire for forgiveness at face value. Love carefully accepts the demonstration of a new pattern of righteousness as a genuine pursuit of godliness. On the assumption that all expressions of new affection on both sides are genuine, the bone broken but now healed should be even stronger than before, the bond of affection deeply cemented by the painful experience of a fracture now mended. Such a pattern of health ought to encourage the further, faithful exercise of both elements of discipline however and whenever appropriate.

The duty of discipline

All this being so, if we are to be faithful to Christ, to one another, and to the world around us, discipline must be part of our life as church members. We are, after all, disciples. Are you ready to discipline and be disciplined?

Do you cheerfully and willingly embrace all aspects of formative discipline? Do you delight yourself in giving and receiving the 'one anothers' of vibrant and vital church membership? Do you enter into all that it means to belong to the body of Christ? Here the preaching and teaching of God's word is central. Here the open, transparent, humble interaction of the saints produces fruit, as we grind off and knock off one another's rough edges, sometimes quite unconsciously, sometimes more deliberately. And, when sin erupts, when transgression stubbornly breaks the bounds of more normal interaction, the church—its members and officers—must step up, individually and corporately.

If you have a position of responsibility within the church of Jesus Christ, are you ready to teach and lead in this matter? Are you ready to 'take point' both in dealing with your own sin and the sin of others? Sin is ugly. Facing it is painful. It may be a duty from which you constitutionally shrink, a responsibility which you view with distaste and distress. A good soldier of Christ must fight the battles that his Commander gives him. There is no prosperity for the church which covers its sin, which neglects the principled cultivation of Christlikeness. There is no true peace in a church which closes ranks to cover treachery within, and which refuses to deal with iniquity. We do not protect the church by pretending that these things do not happen, are not happening, will sort themselves out, or will simply resolve themselves and be forgotten over time. We rather allow a sequence of festering wounds to cripple the body of Christ, leaching her purity, weakening her testimony, covering rather than cleansing her errors, and compromising her very identity. Though written in individual terms, there is a corporate edge to the proverb: 'He who covers his sins will not prosper, but whoever confesses and forsakes them will have mercy' (Prov. 28:13). We cannot be the people who believe in church discipline only until the point at which we actually have to do it.

Are you, as a church member, ready to invest in other believers with a view to growing more like Jesus Christ together and less like the world from which you have been saved? We must proceed with love, with courage, with tenderness (Gal. 6:1), with godly fear (1 Cor. 10:12), with much prayer for wisdom (James 1:5). But we must actually proceed, just as Christ has instructed us. Formative discipline should be our joy, the happy instinct of our renewed nature, both in giving and receiving. We should not have an unhealthy appetite for restorative or corrective discipline; we should never revel in it. Because we live in a fallen world it will sooner or later come to us. We must prepare to meet it, face it with integrity, and respond in righteousness. The uglier and the harder the situation, the more personal its effects, the closer it strikes, the more ready we must be to obey with fierce determination and humble hearts the commands of our Lord. We must be prepared to pay whatever price is necessary to see Christ's name vindicated, his body cleansed, the saints warned, sinners recovered, sin exterminated, and the world sent a clear, bright message about the nature and character of the house of God.

Holiness matters because heaven and hell matter. If we are to be holy and heaven-bound, drawing others on to that bright and upward path, then we must be and live as true disciples of Jesus Christ. God cares enough to provide for the life and health of his church. Do you care enough to pursue it?

BANNER *of* **TRUTH**

The Banner of Truth Trust originated in 1957 in London. The founders believed that much of the best literature of historic Christianity had been allowed to fall into oblivion and that, under God, its recovery could well lead not only to a strengthening of the church, but to true revival.

Interdenominational in vision, this publishing work is now international, and our lists include a number of contemporary authors, together with classics from the past. The translation of these books into many languages is encouraged.

A monthly magazine, *The Banner of Truth*, is also published, and further information about this, and all our other publications, may be found on our website, banneroftruth.org, or by contacting the offices below:

Head Office:
3 Murrayfield Road
Edinburgh
EH12 6EL
United Kingdom
Email: info@banneroftruth.co.uk

North America Office:
610 Alexander Spring Road
Carlisle, PA 17015
United States of America
Email: info@banneroftruth.org